WORLD HABITATS

MOUNTAINS and VOLCANOES

Rose Pipes

A ZOË BOOK

A ZOË BOOK

© 1997 Zoë Books Limited

Devised and produced by
Zoë Books Limited
15 Worthy Lane
Winchester
Hampshire SO23 7AB
England

First published in Great Britain in 1997 by
Zoë Books Limited
15 Worthy Lane
Winchester
Hampshire SO23 7AB

A record of the CIP data is available from the British Library.

ISBN 1 86173 012 8

Printed in Italy by Grafedit SpA
Editor: Kath Davies
Artwork: David Hogg
Map: Sterling Associates
Design & Production: Sterling Associates

Photographic acknowledgments

The publishers wish to acknowledge, with thanks, the following photographic sources:

Environmental Images / Colin Cumming 26; Robert Harding Picture Library / Geoff Renner 16; / Thomas Laird 18; / Michael Jenner 26; The Hutchison Library / Jeremy Horner - cover background; / T.Molins - title page; Impact Photos / Ken Graham 9; / Mark Cator 19; NHPA / Ken Griffiths 22; Philip A. Sauvain 27; South American Pictures / Kimball Morrison 10; / Tony Morrison 12, 13; Still Pictures / Peter Weimann - cover inset br; / Mark Edwards 11; / Claude Thouvenin 20; / Hartmut Schwarzbach 21; TRIP / R Powers 7; / T Mackie 15, 17; / Eric Smith 23, 25; Zefa - cover inset bl, 14, 24, 28.

The publishers have made every effort to trace the copyright holders, but if they have inadvertently overlooked any, they will be pleased to make the necessary arrangement at the first opportunity.

Contents

Where are the world's mountains and volcanoes?

Most of the world's mountains and volcanoes are in places where the outside, or crust, of the earth moves slowly all the time.

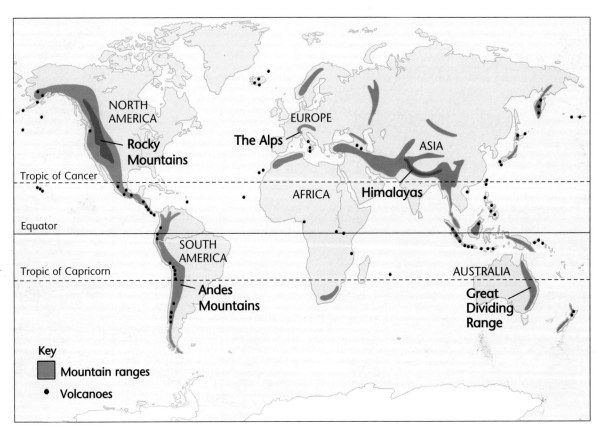

This map of the world shows places where there are mountains and volcanoes.

The world's mountains were formed millions of years ago. Some mountain ranges are under the oceans.

These pictures show two ways in which mountains may be formed.

these two blocks of land slip down

block mountains

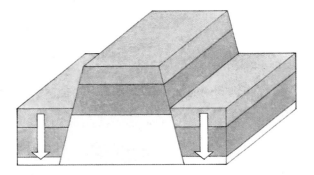

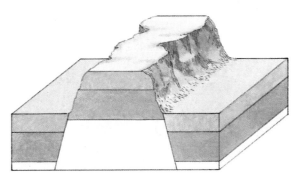

cracks, or faults, in the Earth's crust

fold mountains

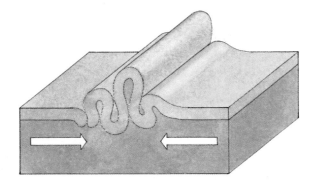

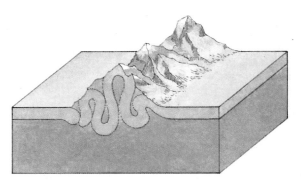

When two parts of the Earth's crust push against each other, the rocks are squeezed together. They are pushed upwards to form fold mountains.

How volcanoes may be formed

Volcanoes come in many shapes and sizes. There are low, flat volcanoes, and tall, cone-shaped ones. Some volcanoes have large hollows, called craters, at the top.

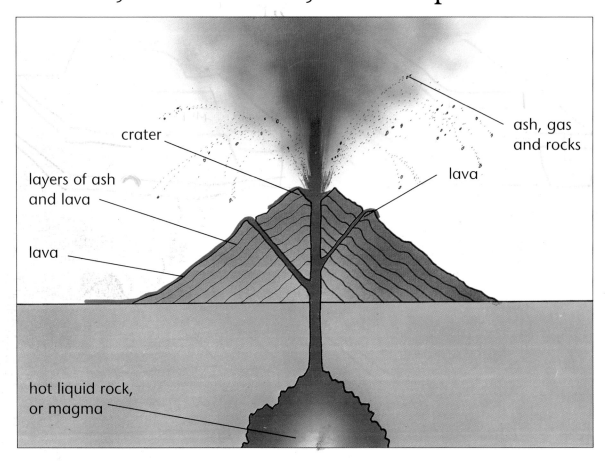

crater

ash, gas and rocks

lava

layers of ash and lava

lava

hot liquid rock, or magma

A volcano forms when hot gases, rocks, **lava** and ash burst out of the ground.

Most volcanoes are very old, but some have formed in the last 100 years. They may form under the oceans and stick up above the water as islands.

Some volcanoes blow up, or erupt, very suddenly. Others may form slowly.

This picture shows red hot lava erupting out of a volcano in Costa Rica.

Life in the mountains

The weather gets colder and the wind is stronger as you climb upwards. Even in hot countries, high mountains may have snow on the top all year round.

These mountains and valleys are in the European Alps. You can see that the land changes from the bottom to the top of the mountains.

Different plants grow at different levels. Trees grow on the lower slopes, and grass and wild flowers grow higher up. Each of these 'layers' is a different **habitat** with its own kinds of wildlife.

The scenery in many mountain areas is very beautiful. People enjoy walking, skiing and climbing there.

Alaska, USA, is a good place to learn to ski. There is plenty of snow here in the winter.

The Andes in South America

The Andes Mountains range is in South America. It is the longest range in the world.

This picture shows the volcano named Cotopaxi. It erupted 50 times between 1742 and 1942. It is the highest **active volcano** in the Andes.

There are many volcanoes in the Andes. The highest volcano is Aconcagua, at 6960 metres. It never erupts, so it is called an **extinct volcano**.

A large area of high, flat land in the mountains is called a plateau. In the Andes, there are many villages, towns and cities on the high plateaux.

The highest capital city in the world is La Paz in Bolivia. It spreads across a plateau in the Andes. People who live there have **adapted** to breathing the thin mountain air.

The Andes Mountains are the home of the largest bird on earth. It is called the condor.

The condor's body is about one metre long and its **wingspan** is about 3 metres.

Mountain rocks may contain gold and other valuable **minerals**. There are huge copper and tin mines in the Andes. People mine tin in Bolivia, and copper in Chile.

Roads and railways carry the minerals down to **ports** on the coast. They also bring tourists up into the high mountains.

These people are Quechua Indians. They are selling goods to people on the mountain trains.

Many Quechua Indians farm land in the mountains. They keep animals such as llamas.

The Rocky Mountains in North America

The Rocky Mountains range is in North America. It stretches from the icy lands of

Some peaks in the Rockies are more than 4000 metres high. There are gaps, or passes, through the mountains. Roads and railways run through these passes. This road is the Icefields Parkway in Alberta, Canada.

Alaska in the north to the dry lands of Mexico in the south.

There are many different habitats in the Rockies. Forests of **coniferous trees** grow on the mountain slopes. Below the forests, there is grassland.

Above the forests, the mountain slopes are bare and steep. Wild goats live there. They have thick hair to keep them warm.

These wild elk are close to the forests. The elk eat leaves, twigs, bark and shoots.

There are some very large **National Parks** and **nature reserves** in the Rockies. People visit them to see the wildlife and the scenery.

Yellowstone was the world's first National Park. It is in Wyoming, USA. This is the Morning Glory Pool. Hot water from deep in the earth brings minerals up to the surface.

Many of North America's largest rivers start in the Rockies. There are hundreds of lakes in the Rockies, too. Some of these lakes are **reservoirs**. Water flows through pipelines from the reservoirs to towns and farms at the foot of the mountains.

There is water everywhere in the Rockies. Streams and waterfalls tumble down the slopes, and rivers flow from the mountains.

The Himalayas in Asia

The world's highest mountains are in the Himalayas, in Asia. The Himalayas are partly in China and partly in Nepal.

The highest peak in the Himalayas is Mount Everest at 8863 metres. You can see it in this picture.

Many climbing expeditions into the Himalayas start in the city of Kathmandu. It is the capital city of Nepal.

Snow and ice cover the tops of the high peaks all year round. The winds here are cold and fierce. No plants or animals can live this high up.

Heavy rain falls on the south-facing slopes of the Himalayas. You can see bushes called giant rhododendrons growing on the slopes.

Some unusual animals live on the mountain slopes above the forests. The bird called the rose-breasted finch lives as high

This snow leopard lives in the Himalayas. People hunted the leopard and at one time, it was in danger of dying out. Now these animals are **protected**.

up as 5500 metres. This is higher than any other songbird in the world.

The Sherpa people used to live by farming and herding animals. Now, many of them work as guides. They take people on long walks, or treks, through the mountains.

Sherpa women carry packs for tourists on a trek in Nepal.

The Great Dividing Range in Australia

The lines of mountain ranges on the eastern side of Australia are called the Great Dividing Range.

In this picture of the Warrumbungle mountains, you can see peaks of very hard volcanic rocks. The softer rocks around the peaks have worn away.

The land on the west side of the Great Dividing Range is much drier than on the east side. Farmers have to water, or irrigate, their crops on the west side.

Tunnels and pipelines carry river water from the Snowy Mountains to the dry farmlands.

There are lakes and reservoirs in the high mountains at the south end of the range. Reservoirs like this one store water. The water flows through pipelines to towns, where people use it as drinking water.

Trees called eucalyptus grow on the mountain slopes. Koalas hang on to the tree branches with their sharp claws, and eat the leaves.

A young koala lives in its mother's pocket, or pouch, for about six months. Animals with pouches are called marsupials.

There are large towns and cities on the coast near the mountains at the south end of the Great Dividing Range.

In summer, people from the towns travel up into the mountains for holidays. It is cooler in the high mountains than on the coast. They can enjoy walking and climbing.

In the winter, people ski in the mountains in the south. Mount Kosciusko is the highest peak, at 2228 metres. It lies in a National Park.

The Alps in Europe

The Alps is the name for the highest mountain range in Europe. It runs from France through Switzerland and Austria into Italy.

This is a **glacier** on Mont Blanc. Its name is *Mer de Glace*, which means Sea of Ice.

The highest peak in the range is Mont Blanc ('white mountain') in the French Alps. It is 4807 metres high. Snow and ice cover the top of Mont Blanc all year round.

Thousands of years ago, ice covered the Alps. Glaciers moved forward very slowly, carving out valleys.

A glacier made this steep-sided valley in the Alps. It is shaped like the letter 'U'. A river now runs through the valley, and there is flat land beside it.

In most Alpine valleys, there are trees on the lower slopes. Above the trees, grass and wild flowers grow in the meadows.

These farms and meadows are in Switzerland. The mountain in the picture is called the Eiger.

Farmers in the Alps make cheeses from the milk of goats and cows. These Alpine cheeses are famous all over Europe.

Many Alpine villages and towns are holiday **resorts**. More people now work in holiday towns than on farms.

Chamonix in France is one of the most famous holiday resorts in Europe. Cable cars take people high up on the slopes of Mont Blanc, near Chamonix.

Glossary

active volcano: a volcano that sometimes blows up, or erupts.

adapted: if a plant or an animal can find everything it needs to live in a place, we say that it has adapted to that place. The animals can find food and shelter, and the plants have enough food in the soil and enough water. Some animals have changed their shape or their colour over a long time, so that they can catch food or hide easily. In high places where the air is thin some people and animals have large hearts which help them to breathe more easily.

coniferous trees: trees which have cones and needle-shaped leaves.

extinct volcano: a volcano that has stopped erupting for ever.

glacier: a thick, tongue-shaped mass of ice. Glaciers form in valleys, and move very slowly downhill.

habitat : the natural home of a plant or animal. Examples of habitats are deserts, forests and grasslands.

lava: very hot, melted rock which flows from deep in the earth up to the surface.

minerals: something which we usually find in rocks, such as gold, copper and tin. Minerals are taken from the earth or rocks by mining.

National Parks: laws protect these lands and their wildlife from harm. These places usually have beautiful scenery and rare wildlife.

nature reserves: an area set aside for wildlife to live in.

ports: towns where ships load and unload their goods. They may be next to rivers, lakes or the sea.

protected: kept safe from changes that would damage the habitat.

reservoirs: lakes which have been specially built or used to store water for people to use.

resorts: places, such as villages or towns, that people visit on holiday.

wingspan: the length across the outstretched wings of a bird.

Index